Franklin Watts Inc
387 Park Avenue South
New York
NY 10016

Library of Congress Cataloging-in-Publication Data
Stephen, R. J.
    Warships / R. J. Stephen.
        p.   cm. — (Picture world)
    Includes index.
    Summary: Describes the structure and the functions of the various kinds of ships used in warfare.
        ISBN 0-531-14013-X
        1. Warships—Juvenile literature.   [1. Warships.]   I. Title.
    II. Series.
    V765.B28   1990   89-36499
    359.3′25—dc20   CIP
                                                                  AC

Printed in Belgium

Series Editor
Norman Barrett

Designed by
K and Co.

Photographs by
Australian Department of
    Defense
Fleet Photographic Unit
Swedish Naval Attache
U.S. Department of Defense
U.S. Navy

Technical Consultant
Bernie Fitzsimons

The Picture World of

Warships

R.J. Stephen

CONTENTS

Franklin Watts

London • New York • Sydney • Toronto

Introduction

The navies of the world are made up of all kinds of warships, from tiny patrol boats to enormous aircraft carriers.

With their heavy guns, warships possess massive firepower for close combat. But even some of the smallest boats carry considerable destructive power in the form of long-range guided missiles.

▽ The main armament of this American cruiser is a launcher for guided missiles. Cruisers are the largest escort vessels for aircraft carriers.

△ A battleship has more big guns than any other warship.

▷ A close-up of a gun on an American destroyer of the Spruance class. These anti-submarine ships are lightly armed, with only one of these medium guns at either end. More important are the weapon systems behind the gun.

Sailing the sea

Most warships are powered by steam turbines, which drive propellers. The steam is produced by oil or nuclear fuel. Some advanced warships are now powered by gas turbines, a cheaper method.

Ships are run from a control room on the bridge. They are navigated and steered automatically with the aid of computers.

▽ Inside the engine room of a warship. Steam produced in boilers spins the turbine wheels to turn the ship's propellers. Gas turbines use hot gases instead of steam.

Life on board

The number of crew on a warship ranges from five on a tugboat to over 6,000 on the largest aircraft carriers. The captain commands the ship assisted by officers.

A sailor's life depends on the type of ship he sails. On large ships, each crew member has a specialized job to do — in the control room or engine room, in the ship's maintenance or living quarters or with aircraft or weapons.

△ Officers look on while the deck crew carry out routine duties. Sailors take pride in keeping all parts of their ship clean and in perfect working order.

△ Ships that carry
planes or helicopters
have a special crew for
looking after the
aircraft.

▽ Crewmen prepare
for a gun-firing
exercise in the fire-
control room of a
frigate.

◁ Scraping the anchor — not everyone's idea of a sailor's job, but someone has to do it!

▷ A more popular job — spraying a symbol on the bridge of a minesweeper to indicate that another mine has been removed.

Masters of the ocean

The most powerful ships afloat are submarines and aircraft carriers. They each perform tasks the other cannot do.

Carriers convey massive air power across the world's oceans. They serve as floating airfields, protected by groups of other ships and submarines. A battle group headed by a large aircraft carrier is a powerful military force.

△ USS *Dwight D. Eisenhower*, a nuclear-powered carrier with a crew of more than 6,000 and capable of carrying nearly 100 combat aircraft.

Nuclear power enables submarines to stay underwater for several months without surfacing.

Hunter-killer, or attack, submarines operate with fleets. They attack enemy warships and help to protect their own aircraft carriers and ships from enemy submarines.

Ballistic missile submarines hide in the depths of the ocean. Their long-range nuclear missiles can destroy whole cities.

▽ The nuclear-powered ballistic missile submarine USS *Andrew Jackson*. Long-range nuclear missiles that can be launched from under the water serve as a threat to prevent an enemy from starting a nuclear war.

Escort vessels

Escort vessels are ships that form part of a battle group, or task force, and help to protect the aircraft carrier. The carrier is also guarded by its own aircraft, and these protect the escort vessels, too.

The chief escort vessels are cruisers, destroyers and frigates, all powerful warships.

▽ A view from the air of the carrier *Carl Vinson*, surrounded by escort vessels of its battle group. These cruisers, destroyers and frigates are not small ships, but they are dwarfed by the carrier.

14

△ USS *Virginia*, a nuclear-powered guided-missile cruiser. These modern cruisers carry anti-submarine rockets and torpedoes, and supersonic missiles that can be fired at aircraft 140 km (87 miles) from the ship.

▷ A Soviet guided-missile cruiser of the Kirov class. These "battle-cruisers" are more than just escort vessels. Second only to carriers in size, they carry more firepower than any other ship afloat.

Destroyers defend carriers and amphibious and merchant ships. They are also used for bombarding enemy shores and for such missions as search and rescue.

◁ HMS *Manchester*, of the British Navy.

▷ The Soviet guided-missile destroyer *Krasny-Krym*.

▽ The American destroyer *John Young*, with guns firing.

▷ A Sea-Cat surface-to-air missile is launched from the deck of a warship. Guided missiles such as these make even the smallest warships a threat to enemy aircraft.

▽ The American guided-missile frigate *Crommelin,* as seen from the deck of a carrier.

Frigates are chiefly used to defend against submarines, but some carry guided missiles for defense against aircraft.

▷ An American frigate, the USS *Brewton*, is escorted into Sydney Harbor during the Australian bicentennial celebrations.

▽ HMS *London*, a guided-missile frigate of the British Navy.

19

Other kinds of warships

Battleships once ruled the seas. But their firepower has been largely replaced by the air power of carriers and the guided missiles and rockets of smaller ships.

The only battleships still in service are four Iowa class ships of the U.S. Navy. These are rebuilt World War II battleships, first launched in the early 1940s.

▷ The battleship *New Jersey*, with some of its 1,600 crew manning the decks, in San Francisco Bay.

▽ An aerial view of *New Jersey*, demonstrating its firepower.

◁ The battleship *Iowa*, with guns ablaze, is a spectacular sight from the air at night.

▽ A replenishment oil tanker (center) refuels a cruiser (left) and a destroyer (right).

Other kinds of warships have their own special jobs to do. Amphibious assault ships land troops, weapons and equipment. Supply ships provide fighting ships with fuel and equipment.

Ships called small combatants operate chiefly in coastal waters. They include minesweepers and minelayers, missile boats and patrol boats.

◁ Marines load a howitzer aboard USS *Guam*, an amphibious assault ship. This class of ship is specially designed to operate helicopters.

▽ The patrol combatant *Tacoma* is in a class of fast boats used for patrol and surveillance missions.

▷ The minesweeper HMS *Dovey*. Minesweepers find and remove underwater explosives. This class of minesweeper, often used in teams, tows special gear for "sweeping" in deep water.

◁ The mine counter-measures vessel HMS *Brecon*. Brecon class minesweepers are the largest warships built of glass reinforced plastic, a material that does not trigger magnetic mines.

▷ Fast attack craft of the Swedish Navy. These speedy Spica class boats, used for attacking surface vessels, are armed with torpedoes and surface-to-surface missiles.

Facts

Pennant numbers

The number painted on a ship's side, or in the case of carriers on its deck, is called its pennant number. The full identification of a ship has a letter or letters before its number, but not all navies have the letter painted on the ship.

These letters depend on which navy the ship belongs to. For example, British submarines have an S before their numbers, while American submarines have SS (diesel-electric submarines), SSN (nuclear-powered) or SSBN (nuclear-powered ballistic missile). In the same way,

frigates are denoted by FF (American) or F (British), destroyers by DD or D. U.S. Navy aircraft carriers are denoted by CV or CVN (nuclear-powered), British carriers by R.

△ This ship flies the flag of the U.S. Navy, which does not have the letters with the number. It is the frigate USS *Koelsch*, designated FF-1049.

△ The pennant number F58 is painted on the side of this ship, which flies a British Navy flag. The number denotes that it is the frigate HMS *Hermione*.

Weight

A warship's weight is usually given as displacement tonnage — the number of long tons of water displaced, or occupied, by the ship. One long ton is equivalent to 1.016 tons.

The biggest warships, the Nimitz class aircraft carriers, have a displacement of 81,600 tons. This rises to 91,487 tons when it is fully laden with aircraft, supplies, fuel and ammunition.

As a general rule, frigates weigh from 1,100 to 3,000 tons, destroyers 3,000–7,000 tons and cruisers over 7,000 tons. Some light patrol boats weigh less than 30 tons.

△ The carrier USS *America* has a displacement of 78,500 tons fully laden. This is the weight of water displaced by the part of the ship underwater.

Naval strengths

The United States and the Soviet Union have by far the world's largest navies. Not including marines, the U.S. Navy has nearly 600,000 personnel, the Soviet Navy 450,000. The Chinese Navy has about 100,000, while the French and British navies have over 60,000 each.

The U.S. and Soviet navies each have more than 30 cruisers, 60 destroyers and 100 frigates. The U.S. Navy has more carriers — 14 attack and 12 helicopter carriers — than the Soviet's 4 and 2. But the Soviet Union has many more submarines — about 75 ballistic missile submarines (SSBNs) and some 300 others to the United States' 36 SSBNs and about 100 others. The Chinese Navy also has more than 100 submarines. The only battleships still in service are the four of the U.S. Navy.

△ The *New Jersey* being towed to the Pacific by tugboats for sea trials. This is one of four World War II battleships rebuilt by the U.S. Navy in the 1980s.

Glossary

Amphibious
Operating on land as well as water. Amphibious assault ships do not themselves operate on land, but carry helicopters and troops that do.

Ballistic missile submarine
A submarine armed with long-range nuclear missiles.

Battle group
A force of ships, usually centered on an aircraft carrier and helping to protect it while the group carries out its mission.

Bridge
The platform above the main deck, from which the captain and his officers control the ship and give directions.

Displacement tonnage
The weight of a ship, given as the number of long tons of water it displaces (1 long ton = 1.016 tons).

Escort vessel
A ship whose chief job is to protect an aircraft carrier.

Guided missile
A weapon that is steered to its target. Some fly under human control, while others are guided by built-in computer.

Nuclear missile
A missile with a nuclear warhead — that is, an atomic bomb.

Nuclear-powered
Driven by nuclear fuel.

Small combatants
Small boats, such as fast attack craft, missile boats and minesweepers, that operate chiefly near coasts.

Supersonic
Faster than sound.

Surveillance
Watching or spying on the enemy.

Turbine
A device that uses a moving fluid, such as water or steam, to produce mechanical energy. Turbines are used to power ships.

Index